For Robert and Femke,
in memory of Gwynne Gay

The Journey to Bethlehem

Chris Molan

LION
Children's Books

SEA of GALILEE

GALILEE

Nazareth

Mediterranean Sea

SAMARIA

River Jordan

JUDEAN WILDERNESS

JUDEA

JERUSALEM

JERICHO

BETHLEHEM

DEAD SEA

NORTH

SOUTH

EGYPT

'In those days a decree went out from Emperor Augustus that all the world should be registered. All went to their own towns to be registered. Joseph also went from the town of Nazareth in Galilee to Judea, to the city of David called Bethlehem, because he was descended from the house and family of David.'

Luke 2:1, 3–4

8

The doves were hungry. Their long and dangerous journey from the north had brought them across the wild sea into Palestine.

Yet, even here in the quiet region of Galilee, they were too late. The grain harvest was over. There was not even one fig left on the trees.

Some village girls were busy grinding the grain into flour. Might there be some grains left? Yes – already one girl was scattering some of the kernels of wheat for them to eat. She knew what it was to be weary. Soon, she was going to have a child.

Here, in the Galilean town of Nazareth,
it was warm, especially in the rafters of the carpenters'
workshop. The doves rested until the following morning.
They awoke to the sound of banging.
Someone was hammering extra hard.

'How will I finish these ploughs on my own, Joseph?' complained one of the men. 'Must you go to Bethlehem?'

'Well, the Emperor Augustus wants to count everyone in his empire. The last thing I want to do is leave Nazareth, what with our little one due at any time now... But Bethlehem is my home town, and Mary must come with me.' Joseph held the wood steady. 'I can finish this plough in the few hours before we go,' he said.

Soon it was busy in the courtyard outside. A donkey was being
loaded with provisions: a jar of oil, bags of olives and figs, cheese
in a cloth, and another bag full of flour…

When all was ready, the woman threw her arms around the girl.
'Go safely, Mary,' she said. 'May no harm come your way.'

'Don't cry, Mother,' said Mary softly. 'God has promised us that
all will be well.'

The old man checked the water-skin, and put a reed-paper scroll into Joseph's hand.

'Stay out of Samaria, Joseph. You must go the longer way. And make sure you don't have to stop in any wild places.'

'You must not worry,' said Joseph. 'God has promised us this precious little one. He is to be a prince. No one – not even Emperor Augustus himself – can prevent it.'

The little road wound down through
olive groves and close to fertile fields. The farmers were
harvesting the last of the olives, to fill the oil jars.

'Look, Joseph!' laughed the girl. 'The doves are heading
south too.'

'They will reach Bethlehem first,' said Joseph with a smile. 'But
soon we will be on the straight Roman road. It begins at Lake Galilee.'

The road they were on was full of
ruts and holes. Men were patching it with stones,
as they did every year.

At Lake Galilee, where the road branched to the right, they stopped to rest.

'Why must we avoid Samaria, Joseph?' asked Mary. Looking out over the calm waters, it was difficult for her to imagine danger.

'Samaritans and Jews have been enemies for a long time,' he replied.

He unrolled the scroll to show Mary.

'See how the road runs down the side of the Jordan valley.

That's where we must go.'

The road through the valley was certainly straight and
well-paved. The Roman army kept it in good repair. Heavy wagons,
some with great stones for building, rumbled up and down.

An army officer raced by in his chariot, and Mary and Joseph
pulled back to avoid him.

As Joseph handed over his money to a tollkeeper, some bored-looking soldiers jostled the donkey. They made Joseph nervous.

The doves were swirling overhead in a great cloud, darkening the sky.

'Look – supper!' shouted one of the soldiers and he bent to find a stone for his sling.

But, just in time, a gust of warm air caught the flock of doves and lifted the birds higher. Quietly, Mary and Joseph slipped away.

In the fields beside the road, farmers were
ploughing and scattering seed. The doves rested and ate
in the newly sown fields. The field-workers cursed them and
tried to catch many of them in nets. But at dusk, when the
workers went home, the flock flew on to the River Jordan
and bathed their damaged wings amongst the reeds.

20

Nearby, Mary and Joseph rested for the night.

Mary bathed her face and cooled her ankles. The child was heavy within her. 'Will we be safe here?' she asked.

'Safer here than in Herod's country,' said Joseph grimly.

The long road led them south down the Jordan Valley.

Suddenly, the roofs of Jericho appeared: Jericho – and King Herod's magnificent winter palace! Only the most important matters could keep Herod in the cold hills of Jerusalem – away from here.

Herod was a very dangerous king, who had schemed and murdered his way to the throne, ruling his own people on behalf of the Romans. He laid heavy taxes on his people to build fortresses and palaces, and to raise money to keep an army.

Fearful that people were plotting against him, he had spies everywhere.

The doves rested in the secret shade of the date palms. Then an angry shout from a palace guard sent them wheeling into the sky.

'Let's get away,' urged Joseph, tugging the donkey up the stony track.

Soon they were entering the Judean wilderness near Jerusalem. It was a rocky deserted place. Neither Herod nor even the Romans could make this road safe. There were bandits, wolves, and storms that whipped at all living things.

Surely, their journey's end must be near? As if in answer, a gust of wind brought the clatter of wings. It lifted the birds high up over the dark hills, towards Jerusalem and – Bethlehem!

At last, with the wilderness safely behind them and the great city of
Jerusalem within sight, Mary and Joseph stopped to rest for the night. As
they awoke, the sun rose over Jerusalem. It shone on Herod's New Temple,
and the fortress beyond it.

Already, smoke was rising from the altar in its inner courtyard. The priests were making sacrifices of sheep and pigeons! The flock of wild doves arose, in alarm.

27

Beyond the temple lay Herod's palace. A ray
of sunlight shone into his room. Suspicious, he glowered
towards the window. 'What new trouble will this day
bring me?' he muttered to the guard.

It was dusk when Joseph tugged the tired donkey
up the narrow way into Bethlehem. Already, the lamps
were being lit.

Wherever Mary and Joseph asked for shelter, there was no room to be had. The inn at the end of the street was their last hope.

'I'm sorry, there's no place here for you and the lady,' said the innkeeper. 'It's been the busiest day of the year.'

His wife smiled at the forlorn travellers as
she stepped down from the roof. Around her, doves
cooed softly.

'A young lady in your condition hardly needs another
night under the stars,' she said firmly. 'Come with me.'

She led the donkey to the back of the building. 'This cave is where the animals sleep,' she announced. 'It's all the shelter we have, but it's dry and there's clean straw for a bed…'

Joseph lit a small oil lamp. Then he laid fresh straw to make a bed for his wife. He also made a bed of straw in the empty manger.

Soon, the baby, the promised one, would be here.

High above the wind-swept hills of Bethlehem the shepherds guarding their sheep looked up in wonder. They had spent the evening worrying about protecting their valuable sheep from thieves and from wolves. But now all of that was forgotten. Surely there never was such a brightly lit night sky?

A strange voice filled the night saying:

'Do not be afraid; for see – I am bringing you good news of great joy for all the people: to you is born this day in the city of David a Saviour, who is the Messiah, the Lord. This will be a sign for you: you will find a child wrapped in bands of cloth and lying in a manger.'

And with that a host of angels filled the sky, singing praises to God.

Leaving everything that might hinder them, even
their flock, the shepherds ran, stumbling uphill towards
Bethlehem. The boy ran ahead of them all.

The glow of an oil lamp
drew him to the cave behind the
inn. There lay a young mother
with a baby.

Meanwhile, in a far-off land, some wise men of great learning had been studying the night sky and noticed that one star was brighter than all the rest. They knew that it meant a great ruler was to be born.

So they set off from the East towards Palestine, eagerly following the star to find him. They carried with them gifts fit for a king.

38

When the travellers reached Jerusalem they visited King Herod.

'A new king has been born in Judea,' they told him.

Worried, the king consulted his advisers. Then he returned to his visitors with the information they needed.

'It is said that he will be born in Bethlehem,' Herod announced. 'Why not seek him there? When you have found him,' he said slyly, 'send me word, so that I may worship him too…'

Every night, the star shone above Bethlehem into the little courtyard of
the family's new home. One evening Mary was singing softly to Jesus – that
was the baby's name. The song was a lullaby of Nazareth. The visitors heard
it, as they came along the starlit road.

What sort of king could this be? – wondered the travellers, unloading their gifts – a prince without guards, or wealth, or strong walls?

They laid their gifts before Jesus. Gold, frankincense and myrrh. Gifts for a prince of peace.

That night the wise men slept badly. They sensed danger in their dreams. Soon after dawn, they departed to their own lands. They never returned to tell Herod where the child was.

For Mary, Joseph and Jesus the journey was not yet over. 'Go to Egypt, quickly,' an angel told Joseph. 'Stay there until the danger is past!'

When Herod found that the wise men had tricked him, his fury knew no bounds. He gave orders that all boys in Bethlehem under the age of two should be killed!

So Mary, Joseph and little Jesus fled
south to the land of Egypt where they
could live in safety. They watched as the
doves settled in the warm fields.

'They will fly north again in the spring,' sighed Joseph.
But we will stay here till it is safe for us to go home.'

'When Herod died, an angel of the Lord suddenly appeared in a dream to Joseph in Egypt and said, "Get up, take the child and his mother, and go to the land of Israel, for those who were seeking the child's life are dead." Then Joseph got up, took the child and his mother, and went to the land of Israel. There he made his home in a town called Nazareth.'

Matthew 2:19–21, 23a

Published by
Lion Publishing plc
Sandy Lane West, Oxford, England
www.lion-publishing.co.uk
ISBN 0 7459 4422 1

First edition 2000
10 9 8 7 6 5 4 3 2 1 0

Acknowledgments
The Scripture quotations contained herein
(pp.7, 34 [Luke 2:10–12] and 44) are from
The New Revised Standard Version of the Bible,
Anglicized Edition, copyright ©1989, 1995 by the
Division of Christian Education of the National Council
of the Churches of Christ in the United States of America,
and are used by permission. All rights reserved.

A catalogue record for this book is available
from the British Library

Typeset in 14/22 Footlight MT Light
Printed and bound in Singapore